Peace of
Mind®

Peace of Mind
Flex Curriculum

Kindergarten

Fifteen engaging, flexible and experiential lessons that equip students with the skills to manage big emotions, learn empathy and compassion, build healthy relationships, and express emotions in American Sign Language.

Linda Ryden
Including original stories, illustrations and videos

Welcome to the Peace of Mind Community!

Questions? Comments?
We'd love to hear from you!

Please visit teachpeaceofmind.org or
contact us at info@TeachPeaceofMind.org.

Peace of Mind Publications

Curriculum

Peace of Mind Core Curriculum for Early Childhood
Peace of Mind Core Curriculum for Grades 1 & 2
Peace of Mind Core Curriculum for Grade 3
Peace of Mind Core Curriculum for Grades 4 & 5
Peace of Mind Core Curriculum for Middle School
Peace of Mind Flex Curriculum for Kindergarten
Peace of Mind Flex Curriculum for Grades 1 & 2
Peace of Mind Flex Curriculum for Grade 3
Peace of Mind Flex Curriculum for Grade 4
Peace of Mind Flex Curriculum for Grades 5-8
Social Justice Lesson Curriculum for Grades 3-5

Storybooks

Henry is Kind
Rosie's Brain / El Cerebro de Rosita
Marleigh is Mindful / Marleigh practica la conciencia plena
Marleigh's Big Feelings
Mason and the Conflict CAT / Mason y el conflicto CAT
Quinn and the Worry Channel
Sergio Sees the Good
Tyaja Uses the Think Test

TeachPeaceofMind.org

Peace of Mind Inc. Washington DC 20015
https://TeachPeaceofMind.org
Copyright 2025 Linda Ryden and Peace of Mind Inc.

Editor: Cheryl Cole Dodwell
Cover and Interior Design: Schwa Design Group
Illustrations, Graphics and Videos: Linda Ryden
Logo: Pittny Creative
ISBN: 979-8-9998662-4-0
LCCN: 2025917683
Published 2025

Peace of Mind Flex Curriculum For Kindergarten

Peace of Mind Flex At-a-Glance

Lesson	Topic	Mindfulness Practice and ASL	Kindness Pal Activity	Materials Needed
	All lessons benefit from a way to show lesson SLIDES and a short video to the class and require your Kindness Pal list. Worksheets and Coloring Sheets are included with the lessons. You will need a chime or Vibra-Tone.			
1	Meet Marleigh and Get Kindness Pals	Four Square Breathing	Kindness Pal Shuffle	Chime or Vibra-Tone Four Square Breathing Coloring Sheet
2	Learn How to Say "Happy" in ASL	Four Square Breathing ASL: Happy	Mirror Game	Happy Coloring Sheet
3	Take Five Breathing with Mason	Take Five Breathing ASL: Happy	Sweet or Salty?	Take Five Coloring Sheet
4	Learn to Say "Sad" in ASL	Take Five Breathing ASL: Sad	Kindness Pal Challenge	Trace Your Hand Take Five Coloring Sheet Sad Coloring Sheet
5	Gravity Hands with Navaneet	Gravity Hands	Switcheroo	Gravity Hands Coloring Sheet
6	Learn to Say "Excited" in ASL	Gravity Hands ASL: Excited	Vote for Favorite Mindfulness Practice	Excited Coloring Sheet
7	Squeeze and Release with August	Squeeze and Release ASL: Excited	Find 5 Red Things	Squeeze and Release Coloring Sheet
8	Learn to Say "Hungry" in ASL	Squeeze and Release ASL: Hungry	Find 5 Blue Things	Hungry Coloring Sheet
9	Flower Breathing with Josie and Cybbie	Flower Breathing ASL: Hungry	Copy the Face	Draw Your Own Flower Breathing coloring sheet
10	Learn to Say "Fine" in ASL	Flower Breathing ASL: Fine	Make the number	Fine Coloring Sheet
11	11. Gratefuls with Peyton	Gratefuls ASL: Fine	Draw 3 things you and your KP are grateful for	Gratefuls Sheet
12	12. Learn to Say "Angry" in ASL	Gratefuls ASL: Angry	Kindness pal challenge - 30 seconds	Angry Coloring Sheet
13	13. Make Up Your Own Breaths	Wave Breathing ASL: Angry	Teach your KP your breath	Make Up Your Own Breath Coloring sheet
14	14. Learn to Say "Loved" in ASL	Wave breathing ASL: Loved	KP Challenge	Loved Coloring Sheet
15	15. Heartfulness	Heartfulness ASL: Loved	Kindness Chain	Heartfulness Coloring sheet

Introduction to the Peace of Mind Peace of Mind Flex Curriculum

Welcome to the Peace of Mind Flex Curriculum! If you are looking for a series of flexible mindfulness-based SEL lessons that can be used daily or weekly, this curriculum is for you! This Flex Curriculum is designed to be used in schools and out-of-school time programs where time or staffing constraints allow only 15-20 minutes for social and emotional learning lessons. Lessons may be broken up into modules and taught over the course of a week.

The Peace of Mind Flex Curriculum is accompanied by a complete set of slides for each lesson. All of the videos and coloring sheets are embedded in the slides for ease of use.

Curriculum Theory of Change

Our Theory of Change (ToC) is the same for both our Flex Curriculum and our Core Curriculum. The ToC includes our Curriculum Pillars, Learning Experiences, Core Teaching Practices, and the Outcomes we hope to see for students. Here it is:

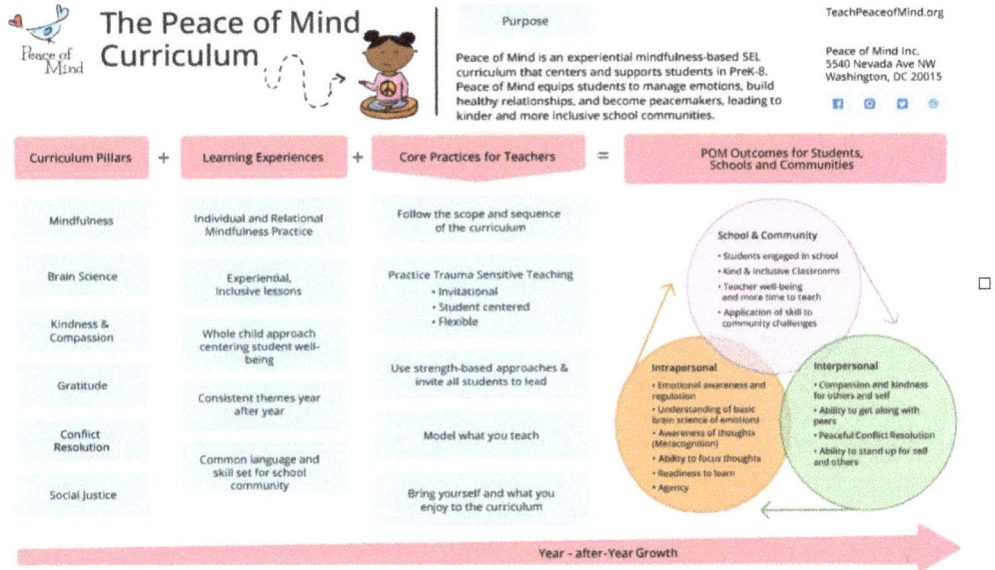

Pillars
The Flex Curriculum is built on Peace of Mind's 6 foundational pillars: Mindfulness, Brain Science, Kindness and Compassion, Gratitude, Conflict Resolution and Social Justice. Engaging and fun, this curriculum uses animated stories and mindfulness practice videos along with interactive discussions and activities to engage students in beginning to notice and manage their emotions and build kind and healthy relationships with others. Lessons include mindfulness

practice, stories, and conversation. Every lesson ends with Kindness Pals, a pair practice that helps students get to know each other and build a caring classroom community in a relatively short time.

Former U.S. Surgeon General Vivek Murthy said that "mental health is the defining public health crisis of our time." The ultimate goal of the Peace of Mind Program is to create a kinder, more peaceful world with and for our children. We begin by helping to create classroom communities where students feel loved and seen. We help children and their grownups learn how to recognize and manage their emotions, how to feel compassion for others and themselves and how to work out conflicts peacefully. We hope that with these personal and interpersonal skills, children will grow up to find peaceful solutions to the most challenging social justice issues of our time.

Learning Experiences

The Flex Curriculum is designed to promote learning experiences that center student well-being and agency while supporting a kind and inclusive classroom and school community. You'll notice that students learn mindfulness not only for themselves, but for their relationships with others.

Each lesson includes three sections:

1. Feelings check-in and American Sign Language
2. Mindful Moment
3. Kindness Pals

Optional worksheets and coloring sheets are included with each lesson.

The curriculum is experiential and inclusive. Peace of Mind helps school communities develop a common language and skill set related to students' own well-being, building healthy relationships, and solving conflicts peacefully.

Outcomes
When taught with fidelity, this series of lessons will help students begin to:

- Increase their self-awareness and self-regulation;

- Begin to regularly practice kindness, compassion and gratitude;

- Build positive relationships with peers and adults;

- Build kind and inclusive classrooms.

Core Teaching Practices

Through our work with partner schools and academic researchers, we have identified five core teaching practices for effective, impactful implementation of Peace of Mind.

1. Follow the Scope and Sequence of the Curriculum

The lesson sequence in this curriculum is designed to give students a foundational set of mindfulness practices to help them begin to manage their emotions and learn to put space between their reactions to a big feeling and their response.

- **Mindfulness**
  In all lessons, students learn an ASL sign and practice mindfulness exercises, building their own tool kit to help them notice, express and begin to manage big emotions. Students experience the effects of each practice personally and begin to discern which practices are most helpful to them.

- **Gratitude**
  We explore gratitude through lessons that help students notice the small good things in their lives.

- **Kindness and Compassion**
  Kindness Pals are assigned each class, and each lesson includes activities for Kindness Pals to do together. The objective of Kindness Pals is to help students get to know each other and practice being kind to each other, even if they are not friends.

2. Practice Trauma Sensitive Teaching

All lessons include three important components of trauma-sensitive teaching:

- **Invitational** - Mindfulness practice is always invitational. While we expect everyone to sit together during the mindful moments, we invite students to choose whether or not to engage with a practice. Students can choose for themselves, but they cannot interfere with someone else's choice. We ask everyone to be respectful of others while making their own decision about whether to do a practice or not. Students are welcome to just sit quietly.

- **Student-centered** - We teach mindfulness practices for students' own well-being. We teach a variety of practices not so students can master them all, but so they can find the ones that work best for them. If a student is having a hard time with a practice, suggest that they choose another one that works better for them.

- **Flexible** - We don't require students to close their eyes or sit in a certain way to practice. If students need to make modifications to a practice (keeping their eyes open or walking quietly in the back of the room, for

example) to help themselves feel comfortable, this is fine as long as their choices do not interfere with others' comfort and safety.

3. Use Strength-Based Approaches

The scripts offered for the lessons use strength-based language: language that focuses on students' abilities, interests and potential, not deficits.

4. Model What You Teach

We know from research and our own experience that modeling what we are teaching is one of the most effective ways of engaging our students in mindfulness practice. Students take their cues from you. You don't have to be an expert in mindfulness, but it is important to model using the practices yourself.

5. Bring Yourself to the Curriculum

Once you are comfortable with the first four core teaching practices, we hope you will be able to bring yourself to the curriculum. If the script isn't quite how you would say things, please adapt so you feel comfortable! If you enjoy singing, bring that in! If you enjoy crafts, make that a part of what you do. If puppets are your thing, they're welcome!

Materials Needed

Slides

The Flex Curriculum is accompanied by a complete set of slides for each lesson. All of the videos and coloring sheets are embedded in the slides for ease of use. Scan the QR code to access the slides.

Storybooks

Marleigh is Mindful is the only storybook you'll need. Marleigh is available as a free read-aloud on the *PoMTV-Kids* YouTube Channel, on the *Peace of Mind website*, and via your favorite bookseller.

Worksheet and Coloring Sheet Copies

You will find related coloring sheets and worksheets right after each lesson. Please print what you need for your class. See "At-A-Glance" to easily find what you need for each lesson.

You may choose to send coloring sheets home after each class so that parents know what their children are learning in Peace Class. Or, you could turn the Coloring Sheets into a book for your students to take home at the end of the session.

Other Materials

These materials are optional but very helpful:

- Ways to Practice Mindfulness Poster
- Mindfulness Card Set
- Chime or bell with a long lasting sound such as a Vibra-Tone

American Sign Language

A new addition to the Peace of Mind Curriculum, American Sign Language is a wonderful tool to use to help all children, regardless of English proficiency, learn about, explore and communicate their emotions. These lessons offer a very basic, simple introduction to expressing emotions in American Sign Language. The ASL included in these lessons is just an introduction to a rich language that can be used to communicate with students who are deaf and hard of hearing or who have other communication challenges.

For more information about learning ASL please visit:

https://www.nad.org/resources/american-sign-language/learning-american-sign-language/

Lesson 1
Meet Marleigh and Get Kindness Pals

Slides:1-10

Note: *Today you are going to be introducing Kindness Pals. You might like to watch this video yourself to help prepare for the lesson: Kindness Pals. You'll notice that all of the lessons have optional scripts. Please feel free to paraphrase, put the scripts in your own words, or just use them as a reference.*

1. Welcome to Peace of Mind!

Introduction to Mindfulness

You might say: *We're going to be learning about something called mindfulness. Have you ever heard of mindfulness before? What do you think it means?* **Invite some answers.**

Mindfulness just means to pay attention. We can pay attention to a lot of different things. Mindfulness can also be about using our breath to help us to take care of ourselves when we are feeling big feelings. How do you breathe when you have been running around for a long time? How do you breathe when you are scared? How do you breathe when you are nervous?

Let's practice a little. I'm going to ring our chime. **Demonstrate the sound of the chime.**

I'm going to ring it again, but this time, I'm going to ask you to either close your eyes or look down into your lap. I'll ring the chime again, and this time I'd like you to try to listen to the sound of the chime until you can't hear it anymore. When you can't hear it anymore, you will raise your hand. Okay?

What will you do when you can't hear the sound of the chime anymore? That's right, raise your hand.

Ring the chime and discuss what it was like to really pay attention to the sound of the chime.

2. Mindful Moment

Today we're going to watch a video about a girl named Marleigh who we're going to be getting to know in Peace of Mind Class. She's a really good dancer, but she gets nervous when she has to perform in front of an audience. Do you ever get nervous?

Marleigh is going to share what she does to feel calmer when she gets nervous. She is going to teach us how to do something called Four Square Breathing. We'll get a chance during the video to try it along with her.

Show Marleigh Four Square Video Marleigh introduces mindfulness and teaches first practice. Pause the video at 1:31 and remind the children that they can try the practice along with Marleigh. Pause again at 1:58 and give the kids a chance to try it again as a group with you. Then finish the video with Marleigh. Don't worry about it being perfect! This is just a chance for the children to start to think about their breathing.

Discuss: *How do you feel?*

3. Kindness Pals

Here's what you'll do: Call out each pair of Kindness Pals from your list, help them move toward each other and sit facing each other. Wait for both students to say "Okay." Notice and comment when they give each other big smiles, and help them decide who should move near whom.

Once all children have been matched up and any absences accounted for, remind them all to listen for the quiet signal when they are chatting with their pal, as that will mean it's time to stop talking and listen for the next directions**.**

The two key things to remember about Kindness Pals: make sure that students get a different pal each time and that they say "Okay!". This might take some practice at the beginning. That's fine. The important thing is for them to learn the lesson that being kind is a choice they can make regardless of how they think they feel about someone. Everytime you talk about it, that message is reinforced.

You might say: *Now we're going to do something fun called Kindness Pals.*

Every class we're going to get a new Kindness Pal. Your Kindness Pal is somebody that you will get to know a little bit better and you get to do kind things for them and they get to do kind things for you. Then next time you'll get a new Kindness Pal. There's one important rule of Kindness Pals. When I tell you who your Kindness Pal is I want you to say **'Okay***!' in a nice friendly way. Let's try that together!*

Are you always going to feel really excited about who you got? Maybe not. And that's okay. But how do you think we will make our Kindness pal feel if we say 'Aw!' or 'Rats!' or 'But I wanted Lily!' That's right, they'll feel really bad. Since this is your Kindness Pal it's your job to be kind to them - just for one day. So the first kind thing you're going to do for them is to say "Okay!"

Skill 1: Responding with "Okay" and a smile
In just a minute, I will call out two names, and those students I call will be each other's Kindness Pal. After I read their names everyone will say "Okay!"

Skill 2: How to face each other
After I call out all the pals, you will move to sit next to each other and you will face each other. To face each other just means your faces are looking at each other.

Turn to one student and point your body at that student. Then let your attention and body wander away and ask the students if you are still facing your "pal." Emphasize that they don't have to look each other in the eyes (uncomfortable for some students) but just be facing each other. **Turn your body back** to the student and emphasize this is how we face each other. Once you've established these expectations you are ready to start the first Kindness Pal session.

Assign Kindness pals as described above.

Kindness Pals Activity: Kindness Pal Shuffle
Let's play a game. This game is called Kindness Pal Shuffle. A few minutes ago we learned how to get a new kindness pal and how to say "okay" so everyone has fun. Now we are going to practice getting together with a Kindness Pal by playing a game.

In a few moments, I am going to give you a new Kindness Pal, you will say "okay!"

When I say "go", you will stand up and move to be next to your partner just like this. (demonstrate).

Then you will sit knee to knee, facing your partner just like I showed you earlier and give your partner a smile or high five.

When I ring the chime everyone will come safely back to the circle. The quicker we can get together with our partners and return to the circle, the more rounds we can play!

Everybody ready?

Play 3 rounds or as many as you have time for.

4. Closing

Let's take a moment to think about something kind you could do for your Kindness pal today. You can close your eyes if you want to. **Wait.**

Ask*: Who has an idea of what you might do?* **Invite** a few answers.

Thanks for a great class, everyone!
Ring a bell or chime if you have one.

Four Square Breathing

Lesson 2
Learn How to Say "Happy" in ASL

Slides: 11-24

> **Note:** *A new addition to the Peace of Mind Curriculum, American Sign Language is a wonderful tool to use to help all children, regardless of English proficiency, learn about, explore and communicate their emotions. These lessons offer a very basic, simple introduction to expressing emotions in American Sign Language. The ASL included in these lessons is just an introduction to a rich language that can be used to communicate with students who are deaf and hard of hearing or who have other communication challenges. For more information about learning ASL please visit: https://www.nad.org/resources/american-sign-language/learning-american-sign-language/*

1. Feelings Check-in and American Sign Language (ASL)

You might say: *We're going to be learning a new way to share our feelings with each other called American Sign Language or ASL. ASL is a visual language - a language that we see with our eyes instead of listening to with our ears.*

When we use ASL, we use our faces, hand signals and body movements instead of saying words with our voices. Most of the people who use ASL are deaf, which means that they cannot hear with their ears. Some are hard of hearing, which means they have trouble hearing with their ears. But lots of other people use it too. We're going to use it to share our feelings with each other.

We're going to start out by learning how to say "happy." How do you feel in your body when you are happy?

Choose a few volunteers to demonstrate what "happy" looks like.

Let's watch a video of one of the Peace of Mind students showing us how to sign "happy." **Happy Video (the video is in the slides)**

ASL Practice
Have everyone try to say "happy" in ASL. Point out that the sign for "happy" involves our faces, hand gestures and body motions. Ask them if the sign for "happy" matches the way that they feel when they are happy.

2. Mindful Moment

You might say: *Now let's practice some Mindful Listening like we did last time.*

I'm going to ring this bell (or chime or whatever you have). I'll ring it one time while you are looking at it and then we'll try to listen to it with our eyes closed or looking down.

Ring the bell for the class.

Okay now let's get into our Mindful Bodies. You can imagine that you have a little zipper going from your belly button to your chin. Imagine that you are zipping up and sitting up a little straighter. If that is too straight for you, then unzip a little until you find your comfy, sort of straight position.

Another part of being in your Mindful Body is deciding what to do with your eyes. Closing your eyes can help you to focus on things like sounds or your breath. If you don't feel comfortable closing your eyes, you could just decide to look down into your lap. It's up to you!

Close your eyes or look down. This time when I ring the bell, try to listen to the whole sound and then raise your hand when you can't hear it anymore.

Ring the bell again. Wait for the last student to raise their hand.
Okay, now you may open your eyes or look up.

Ask:
- What did you notice about the sound?
- Were you able to keep your mind focused on the sound? Or did you start thinking about something else?

Conclude by saying*: If your mind wandered away instead of listening to the bell don't worry! That is perfectly normal. That's what minds do sometimes. The more we practice, the easier it will be to stay focused on the sound.*

> **Note:** *Don't stress about having all kids get into picture perfect mindful bodies! Very few kids will actually stay in their mindful bodies for long if at all. Inviting them to get into their Mindful Bodies is a helpful way to make a transition into what you are doing and to help them practice for the future. If a child is sitting*

with their eyes wide open, that's fine. I usually ask the kids not to look at each other to give everyone a little privacy. For some kids, closing their eyes can be triggering, so it's very important to give kids plenty of options and leeway. It's important for the teacher to always keep your eyes open so that you can keep track of what is happening. The children will probably find it reassuring.

Four Square Breathing Review

Ask if anybody remembers how to do Four Square Breathing. Have them demonstrate for the class.

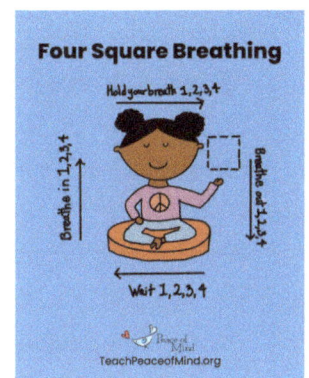

Practice Four Square Breathing as a class. You can play the Marleigh video again or you can lead it on your own. If you choose to lead the practice you can say:

 Let's get into our mindful bodies. Let's close our eyes **or** *look down. Let's take 3 deep Four Square Breaths.*

Lead the class in Four Square Breathing

Say: *Let's listen to the sound of the chime. When you can't hear the sound anymore you can open your eyes or look up.*

Ring the chime.

3. Kindness Pals

Assign New Kindness Pals

You can make a list ahead of time, or put their names on popsicle sticks and pull them randomly out of a jar; however you want to do it is fine.

Call out each pair of Kindness Pals from your list, help them move toward each other and sit facing each other as described above. Wait for both students to say "Okay." Notice and comment when they give each other big smiles, and help them decide who should move near whom. Make sure they are in a good listening position as described above.

Once all children have been matched up and any absences accounted for, remind them all to listen for the quiet signal when they are chatting with their pal, as that will mean it's time to stop talking and listen for the next directions.

You might say: *Remember, every class we're going to get a new Kindness Pal. Your Kindness Pal is somebody that you will get to know a little bit better and you get to do kind things for them. Then next time you'll get a new Kindness Pal. There's one important rule of Kindness Pals. Does anybody remember what it is?*

That's right. When I tell you who your Kindness Pal is, I want you to say "Okay!" in a nice friendly way.

Kindness Pal Activity: The Mirror Game

You might say: *Now we're going to do an activity with your Kindness Pal.*

The first thing we will always do with our pal is to give each other a friendly greeting. A friendly greeting could be a high five, a handshake, a "hello, how are you?" or a fist bump. It could be all of those things.

Now we're going to play the Mirror Game with our Pals. We're going to be moving mindfully and really focusing on what our Kindness Pal is doing. What do you think it means to move mindfully? **Take a few answers.**

You are going to take turns being the leader and doing slow movements with your body. The first leader will be the first name I called first when we paired up. Your Kindness Pal will try to be your reflection in the mirror and do the exact same movements. After one minute I will ask you to switch and the other person will be the leader.

Choose a volunteer to demonstrate the Mirror Game with you and then let them try it with their Kindness Pals for a few minutes.

4. **Optional Drawing Activity**

   Think about how you feel when you are happy. Draw what you look like when you are happy. Think about your face, your hands, and your body movements.

5. Closing

Let's take a moment to think about something kind you could do for your Kindness pal today. You can close your eyes if you want to. **Wait.**

Ask: *Who has an idea of what you might do?* **Invite** a few answers.

Thanks for a great class, everyone!

Ring a bell or chime if you have one.

What do you look like when you are happy?

Lesson 3
Take Five Breathing with Mason

Slides: 25-36

1. Feelings Check-in and ASL Review

ASL Review

You might say: *Let's see who remembers how to say "happy" in ASL. Ask for some children to demonstrate for the class. Remind them that the sign for "happy" (two open hands, palms facing toward your body, brushing up two times) also involves a happy look on your face. You can't make the "happy" sign in ASL with a sad or bored look on your face. Ask everyone to try it that way.*

Feelings Check-in

Now let's do a feelings check in. Take a moment to notice how you are feeling right now.

There are lots of ways to feel and you might feel more than one way. Right now I feel happy and excited (or however you feel). Any way that you feel is fine.

Okay, let's see how you are feeling. You can raise your hand as many times as you want. It's okay to have lots of different feelings.

*Raise your hand or use the sign for "happy" if you are feeling **happy**. Raise your hand if you are feeling **sad**. Raise your hand if you are feeling **excited**. Raise your hand if you are feeling **hungry**. Raise your hand if you are feeling **fine**. Raise your hand if you are feeling **angry**. Raise your hand if you are feeling **loved**. We're going to learn how to say all of these feelings in ASL!*

2. Mindful Moment

Today we're going to learn how to do mindfulness with Marleigh's little brother Mason. The practice we'll be learning is called Take Five Breathing. **Watch the video**. Pause the video at 1:43 and encourage the children to try Take Five Breathing with Mason and Marleigh.

Ask: *What did you notice?*

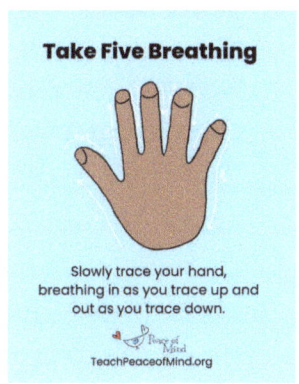

3. Kindness Pals

Assign New Kindness Pals

You might say: *It's time to get our new Kindness Pals! There's one important rule of Kindness Pals. Does anybody remember what it is? When I tell you who your Kindness Pal is I want you to say "Okay!" in a nice friendly way.*

Kindness Pal Activity: Our Favorite Foods

When I say go, you're going to find your Kindness Pal and talk about food!

Call out each pair of Kindness Pals from your list, help them move toward each other and sit facing each other as described above. Wait for both students to say "Okay." Notice and comment when they give each other big smiles, and help them decide who should move near whom. Make sure they are in a good listening position as described above.

Once all children have been matched up and any absences accounted for, remind them all to listen for the quiet signal when they are chatting with their pal, as that will mean it's time to stop talking and listen for the next directions.

The first thing we will always do with our pal is to give each other a friendly greeting. A friendly greeting could be a high five, a handshake, a "hello, how are you?" or a fist bump. It could be all of those things.

Now, when I say go, take turns asking each other what your favorite foods to eat for breakfast, lunch, dinner and dessert are. You've got one minute! Go!"

Share Out
You might say: *Now you get to vote with your feet! This corner is for people who like sweet foods the best. The other corner is for people who like salty foods the best. Ready? When I say go, everyone who likes sweet food best will go to this corner. Everyone who likes salty food best will go to this corner. Go!*

4. Optional Coloring Activity

Ask students to think about times when they could use Take Five Breathing. Have them color in the Take Five Coloring Sheet below.

5. Closing

Let's take a moment to think about something kind you could do for your Kindness pal today. You can close your eyes if you want to. **Wait.**

Ask: *Who has an idea of what you might do?* **Invite** *a few answers.*

Thanks for a great class, everyone!

Ring a bell or chime if you have one.

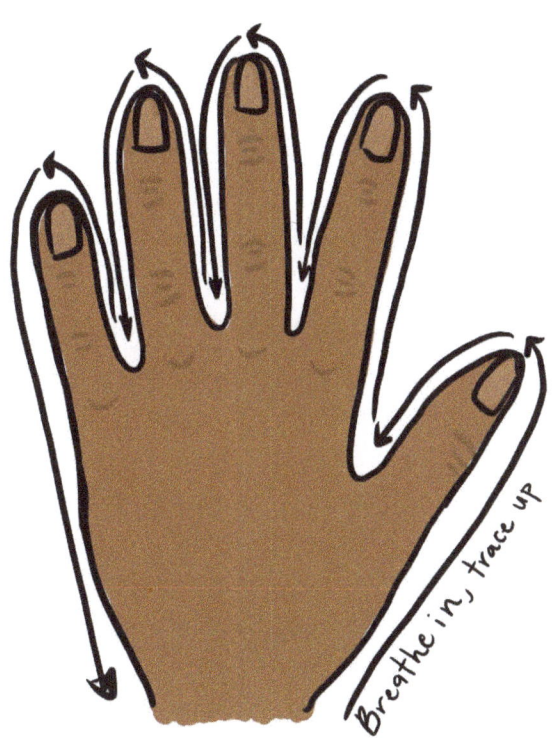

Breathe in, trace up

Take Five Breathing

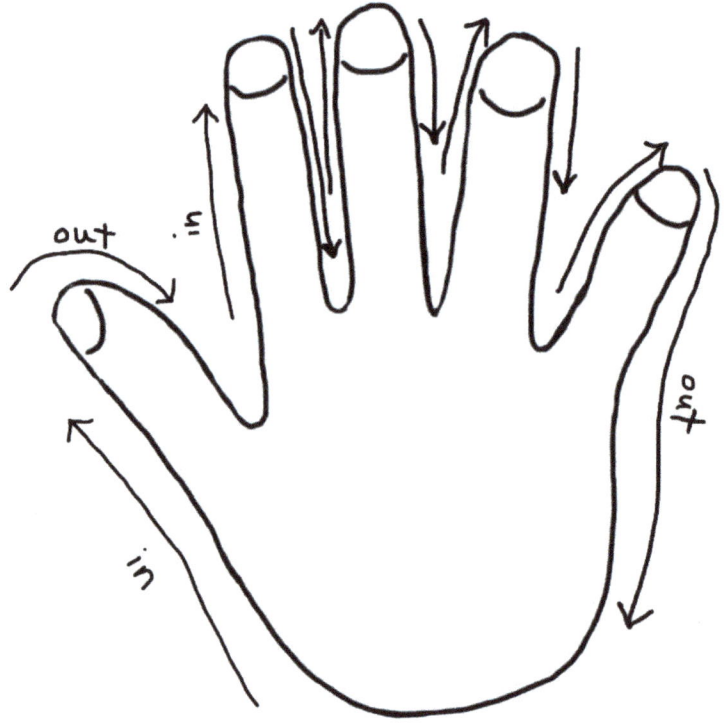

Slowly trace your hand breathing in as you trace up and out as you trace down.

Lesson 4
Learn How to Say "Sad" in ASL

Slides 37- 46

1. Feelings Check-in and ASL Review

ASL Review

You might say: *Let's see who remembers how to say "happy" in ASL.* Ask for some children to demonstrate for the class. Remind them that the sign for "happy" (two open hands, palms facing toward your body, brushing up two times) also involves a happy look on your face. You can't make the "happy" sign in ASL with a sad or bored look on your face. Ask everyone to try it that way.

ASL

*Today we are going to learn another way to share a feeling in ASL. We're going to learn how to say **"sad"**. What does it feel like in your body when you are sad? Where do you feel it?*

To show someone that you are sad in ASL, you need to have a sad look on your face - let's practice that. Then you are going to take your hands with the palms facing in and sort of make a little curtain going down over your face. Let's watch a video of a Peace of Mind student showing how to say "sad". **Sad Video**

Feelings Check-in

Now let's do a feelings check in. Take a moment to notice how you are feeling right now. There are lots of ways to feel and you might feel more than one way. Right now I feel happy and excited (or however you feel). Any way that you feel is fine.

Okay so let's see how you are feeling. You can raise your hand as many times as you want. It's okay to have lots of different feelings.

*Raise your hand or use the sign for "happy" if you are feeling **happy**. Raise your hand or use the sign for "sad" if you are feeling **sad**. Raise your hand if you are feeling **excited**. Raise your hand if you are feeling **hungry**. Raise your hand if you are feeling **fine**. Raise your hand if you are feeling **angry**. Raise your hand if you are feeling **loved**.*

2. Mindful Moment

You might say: *Thanks for sharing how you are feeling today. Who remembers our mindful breathing activity from last time? Yes it was Take Five Breathing! Who can show us how to do Take Five Breathing?*

> **Note**: *You can replay the Marleigh is Mindful video of Take Five Breathing and stop the video to do the practice with Marleigh and Mason, or you can look at it in the book Marleigh is Mindful. And/or you can lead the practice yourself.*

If you want to lead the practice yourself: *Let's get into our mindful bodies. Let's close our eyes OR look down. Let's take 5 deep breaths using Take Five Breathing.*

Ring the chime. You can ring the chime when you are finished and say: *Let's listen to the sound of the bell. When you can't hear it anymore you can open your eyes if they are closed or look up.*

Ask: *What did you notice?*

3. Kindness Pals

Assign Kindness Pals - remind the kids to say "Okay!" You can make a list ahead of time, or put their names on popsicle sticks and pull them randomly out of a jar, however you want to do them is fine. Just make sure that they get a different child each time and that they say "Okay!"

Kindness Pal Activity: Commonalities
You might say: *Today we're going to find out what we have in common. Having something in common with someone means that something is the same about you. Maybe you both like the same kind of ice cream, or you both like to play with blocks. When I say "Go!" you are going to ask your Kindness Pal:*

- What is your favorite ice cream flavor?
- What is your favorite color?
- What is your favorite animal?

See if you can try to remember what your Kindness Pal said.

4. Optional Drawing Activity

Think about how you feel when you are sad. Draw what you look like when you are sad. Think about your face, your hands, and your body movements.

5. Closing

Let's take a moment to think about something kind you could do for your Kindness pal today. You can close your eyes if you want to. **Wait.**

Ask*: Who has an idea of what you might do?* **Invite** *a few answers.*

Thanks for a great class, everyone!

Ring a bell or chime if you have one.

What do you look like when you are sad?

Lesson 5
Gravity Hands with Navaneet

Slides: 48-58

1. Feelings Check-in and ASL Review

ASL Review

You might say: *Let's see who remembers how to say "happy" in ASL.* Ask for some children to demonstrate for the class. Remind them that the sign for "happy" (two open hands, palms facing toward your body, brushing up two times) also involves a happy look on your face. You can't make the "happy" sign in ASL with a sad or bored look on your face. Ask everyone to try it that way.

Say: *Let's see who remembers how to say "Sad" in ASL.* Ask for some children to demonstrate for the class. Remind them that the sign for "sad" (two open hands, palms facing in, making a little curtain going down over your face) also involves a sad look on your face. You can't make the "sad" sign in ASL with a happy or excited look on your face. Ask everyone to try it that way.

Feelings Check-in

Now let's do a feelings check in. Take a moment to notice how you are feeling right now. There are lots of ways to feel and you might feel more than one way. Right now I feel happy and excited (or however you feel). *Any way that you feel is fine.*

Let's see how you are feeling. You can raise your hand as many times as you want. It's okay to have lots of different feelings.

Raise your hand or use the sign for "happy" if you are feeling **happy**. *Raise your hand or use the sign for "sad" if you are feeling* **sad**. *Raise your hand if you are feeling* **excited**. *Raise your hand if you are feeling* **hungry**. *Raise your hand if you are feeling* **fine**. *Raise your hand if you are feeling* **angry**. *Raise your hand if you are feeling* **loved**.

2. Mindful Moment

 Ring the chime for some mindful listening practice (see Lessons 1 and 2)

Today we are going to learn a new mindfulness practice with Marleigh's friend Navaneet. It's called **Gravity Hands**.

Watch the video. Pause the video at 1:36 and encourage the children to try Gravity Hands with Marleigh and Navaneet.

Ask: What did you notice?

3. Assign New Kindness Pals (see Lesson 2)

Okay it's time to get our new Kindness Pals! There's one important rule of Kindness Pals. Does anybody remember what it is? When I tell you who your Kindness Pal is, I want you to say "Okay!" in a nice friendly way.

Kindness Pal Activity: Switcheroo

When I say "Go!" you're going to find your Kindness Pal and you're going to play Switcheroo.

Choose a volunteer to model how to play the game. Model this a few times if necessary.

You and your partner will look at each other for one minute, then turn your backs to each other and switch one thing - like take off your glasses, untie your shoe, change your hairstyle, roll up or down your sleeve, untuck your shirt… Then when I say "Go!," you'll turn around and take turns guessing what has changed about your partner. Ready? Go!

If they seem ready, you can up the challenge by changing two things.

4. Optional Coloring Activity

Ask students to think about times when they could use Gravity Hands. Have them color in the Gravity Hands Coloring Sheet below.

5. Closing

Let's take a moment to think about something kind you could do for your Kindness pal today. You can close your eyes if you want to. **Wait.**
Ask: *Who has an idea of what you might do?* **Invite** a few answers.
Thanks for a great class, everyone!
Ring a bell or chime if you have one.

Gravity Hands

Slowly move your hands up
and down as you breathe in
and out.

Lesson 6
Learn how to say "Excited" in ASL

Slides: 59-70

1. Feelings Check-in and ASL Review

ASL Review

Ask some students to demonstrate how to say "happy" and "sad" in ASL.

ASL

You might say: *Today we are going to learn another way to share a feeling in ASL. We're going to learn how to say "**excited**". What does it feel like in your body when you are excited? Where do you feel it?*

To show someone that you are excited in ASL you need to have an excited look on your face - let's practice that.

Then you are going to take your hands with the palms facing in, with your middle finger pointing toward your palm and your other fingers pointing up and bring them in front of your shoulders and make little circles going in opposite directions. Let's watch a video of a Peace of Mind student showing how to say "excited" in ASL. **Excited Video**

Feelings Check-in

Now let's do a feelings check in. Take a moment to notice how you are feeling right now. There are lots of ways to feel and you might feel more than one way. Right now I feel happy and excited (or however you feel). Any way that you feel is fine.

Let's see how you are feeling. You can raise your hand as many times as you want. It's okay to have lots of different feelings.

*Raise your hand or use the sign for "happy" if you are feeling **happy**. Raise your hand or use the sign for "sad" if you are feeling **sad**. Raise your hand or use the sign for "excited" if you are feeling **excited**. Raise your hand if you are feeling **hungry**. Raise your hand if you are feeling **fine**. Raise your hand if you are feeling **angry**. Raise your hand if you are feeling **loved**.*

2. Mindful Moment

Who remembers our mindful breathing activity from last time? Yes it was Gravity Hands! Who can show us how to do Gravity Hands?

You can replay the Marleigh is Mindful video of Gravity Hands, or you can look at it in the book *Marleigh is Mindful*.

Then you can lead the practice: *Let's get into our mindful bodies. Let's close our eyes OR look down. Let's take 5 deep breaths using Gravity Hands.*

Ring the chime when you are finished and say: Let's listen to the sound of the bell. When you can't hear it anymore you can open your eyes if they are closed or look up.

Ask: *What did you notice?*

Kindness Pals
Assign New Kindness Pals as in Lesson 2.
You might say: *Okay it's time to get our new Kindness Pals! There's one important rule of Kindness Pals. Does anybody remember what it is? When I tell you who your Kindness Pal is I want you to say "Okay!" in a nice friendly way.*

Kindness Pal Activity: **Vote for Your Favorite Practice**
When I say "Go!," you're going to find your Kindness Pal and tell each other what your favorite mindfulness practice is so far. Ask your Kindness Pal why they like that one the best.

Vote with your feet
Label sections of the room for each mindfulness practice we've learned so far and ask them to go stand with the one they like the best. Sometimes picking a favorite can be tricky for younger learners. Let them know it does not have to be their all time favorite, they can just pick one they like today or want to use soon.

3. Optional Drawing Activity

Think about how you feel when you are excited. Draw what you look like when you are excited. Think about your face, your hands, and your body movements.

4. Closing

Let's take a moment to think about something kind you could do for your Kindness pal today. You can close your eyes if you want to. **Wait.**

Ask: *Who has an idea of what you might do?* **Invite** *a few answers.*

Thanks for a great class, everyone!

Ring a bell or chime if you have one.

What do you look like when you are excited?

Lesson 7
Squeeze and Release with August

Slides: 71-81

1. Feelings Check-in and ASL Review

ASL Review
Ask some students to demonstrate how to say "happy", "sad" and "excited" in ASL.

Feelings Check-in
You might say: *Now let's do a feelings check in. Take a moment to notice how you are feeling right now. There are lots of ways to feel and you might feel more than one way. Right now I feel happy and excited (or however you feel). Any way that you feel is fine.*

Let's see how you are feeling. You can raise your hand as many times as you want. It's okay to have lots of different feelings.

*Raise your hand or use the sign for "happy" if you are feeling **happy**. Raise your hand or use the sign for "sad" if you are feeling **sad**. Raise your hand or use the sign for "excited" if you are feeling **excited**. Raise your hand if you are feeling **hungry**. Raise your hand if you are feeling **fine**. Raise your hand if you are feeling **angry**. Raise your hand if you are feeling **loved**.*

2. Mindful Moment

You might say: *Today we're going to learn more about mindfulness with Marleigh's friend August. We'll learn a new practice called **Squeeze and Release**. **Watch the video**. Pause the video when Marleigh says "Let's try it together" and you can lead the practice. Finish the video.*

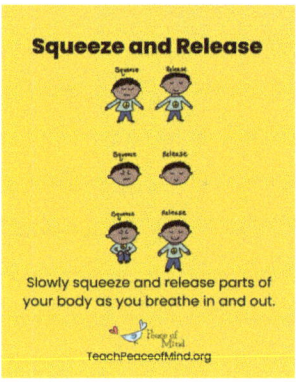

Let's get into our mindful bodies. Let's close our eyes OR look down. Let's take 5 deep breaths using **Squeeze and Release.**

Ring the chime when you are finished and say: Let's listen to the sound of the bell. When you can't hear it anymore you can open your eyes if they are closed or look up.

Ask: *What did you notice?*

3. Kindness Pals

Assign New Kindness Pals as in Lesson 2

You might say: *It's time to get our new Kindness Pals! There's one important rule of Kindness Pals. Does anybody remember what it is? When I tell you who your Kindness Pal is, I want you to say "Okay!" in a nice friendly way.*

Kindness Pal Activity: Find 5 Red Things

When I say "Go!," you're going to find your Kindness Pal and you are going to walk around the room and try to find 5 red things together. Then you'll tell each other what your favorite red thing is.

4. Optional Coloring Activity

Ask students to think about times when they could use Squeeze and Release. Have them color in the Squeeze and Release Coloring Sheet below.

5. Closing

Let's take a moment to think about something kind you could do for your Kindness pal today. You can close your eyes if you want to. **Wait.**

Ask: *Who has an idea of what you might do?* **Invite** a few answers.

Thanks for a great class, everyone!

Ring a bell or chime if you have one.

Squeeze and Release

Slowly squeeze and release parts of your body as you breathe in and out

Lesson 8
Learn to Say "Hungry" in ASL

Slides: 82-92

1. Feelings Check-in and ASL Review

ASL Review

Ask some students to demonstrate how to say "happy", "sad" and "excited" in ASL.

ASL

You might say: *Today we are going to learn another way to share a feeling in ASL. We're going to learn how to say "**hungry**". What does it feel like in your body when you are hungry? Where do you feel it?*

To show someone that you are hungry in ASL you need to have a hungry look on your face - let's practice that. Then you are going to choose one hand and bring your fingers and your thumb together. Then you're going to draw a line from your throat to your tummy with that hand two times. Let's watch a video of a Peace of Mind student showing how to say "Hungry" in ASL. **Hungry Video**

Feelings Check-in

Now let's do a feelings check in. Take a moment to notice how you are feeling right now. There are lots of ways to feel and you might feel more than one way. Right now I feel happy and excited (or however you feel). Any way that you feel is fine.

Let's see how you are feeling. You can raise your hand as many times as you want. It's okay to have lots of different feelings.

*Raise your hand or use the sign for "happy" if you are feeling **happy**. Raise your hand or use the sign for "sad" if you are feeling **sad**. Raise your hand or use the sign for "excited" if you are feeling **excited**. Raise your hand or use the sign for "hungry" if you are feeling **hungry**. Raise your hand if you are feeling **fine**. Raise your hand if you are feeling **angry**. Raise your hand if you are feeling **loved**.*

2. Mindful Moment

You might say: *Who remembers our mindfulness activity from last time? Yes it was Squeeze and Release! Who can show us how to do Squeeze and Release?*

You can replay the Marleigh is Mindful video of Squeeze and Release, or you can look at it in the book *Marleigh is Mindful*. Then you can lead the practice: *Let's get into our mindful bodies. Let's close our eyes OR look down. Let's take 3 deep breaths using Squeeze and Release.*

Ring the chime when you are finished and say: *Let's listen to the sound of the bell. When you can't hear it anymore you can open your eyes if they are closed or look up.*
Ask: *What did you notice?*

3. Kindness Pals

Assign New Kindness Pals as in Lesson 2
You might say: *Okay it's time to get our new Kindness Pals! There's one important rule of Kindness Pals. Does anybody remember what it is? When I tell you who your Kindness Pal is I want you to say "Okay!" in a nice friendly way.*

Kindness Pal Activity: Find Five Blue Things
Okay when I say "go," you're going to find your Kindness Pal and you are going to walk around the room and try to find 5 blue things together. Then you'll tell each other what your favorite blue thing is.

4. Optional Drawing Activity

Ask students to think about how they feel when they are hungry. Invite them to draw what they look like when they are hungry, prompting them to think about their face, hands, and body movements.

5. Closing

Let's take a moment to think about something kind you could do for your Kindness pal today. You can close your eyes if you want to. **Wait.**
Ask: *Who has an idea of what you might do?* **Invite** a few answers.
Thanks for a great class, everyone!
Ring a bell or chime if you have one.

What do you look like when you are hungry?

Lesson 9
Flower Breathing with Josie and Cybbie

Slides: 93-102

1. Feelings Check-in and ASL Review

ASL Review
Ask some students to demonstrate how to say "happy", "sad", excited" and "hungry" in ASL.

Feelings Check-in
You might say: *Now let's do a feelings check in. Take a moment to notice how you are feeling right now. There are lots of ways to feel and you might feel more than one way. Right now I feel happy and excited (or however you feel). Any way that you feel is fine.*

Let's see how you are feeling. You can raise your hand as many times as you want. It's okay to have lots of different feelings.

*Raise your hand or use the sign for "happy" if you are feeling **happy**. Raise your hand or use the sign for "sad" if you are feeling **sad**. Raise your hand or use the sign for "excited" if you are feeling **excited**. Raise your hand or use the sign for "hungry" if you are feeling **hungry**. Raise your hand if you are feeling **fine**. Raise your hand if you are feeling **angry**. Raise your hand if you are feeling **loved**.*

2. Mindful Moment

You might say: *Today we're going to learn more about mindfulness with Marleigh's friends Josie and Cybbie. Our new practice is called **Flower Breathing**.*

Pause the video when Marleigh says "Let's try it together" and you can lead the practice: Let's get into our mindful bodies. Let's close our eyes OR look down. Let's take 3 deep breaths using Flower Breathing.

Let's listen to the sound of the bell. When you can't hear it anymore you can open your eyes if they are closed or look up.

Finish the video.

Ask: *What did you notice?*

3. Kindness Pals

Assign New Kindness Pals as in Lesson 2

You might say: *Okay it's time to get our new Kindness Pals! There's one important rule of Kindness Pals. Does anybody remember what it is? When I tell you who your Kindness Pal is I want you to say "Okay!" in a nice friendly way and move mindfully to sit next to them.*

Kindness Pal Activity: Copy The Face Game

You and your Kindness Pal are going to take turns copying each other as you make a face. Make a happy face, a sad face, an excited face, an angry face, a silly face, whatever kind of face you want and your Kindness Pal will try to copy it like you are looking in a mirror. Then you'll switch!

4. Optional Coloring Activity

Ask students to think about times when they could use Flower Breathing. Have them color in the Coloring Sheet below.

5. Closing

Let's take a moment to think about something kind you could do for your Kindness pal today. You can close your eyes if you want to. **Wait.**

Ask: *Who has an idea of what you might do?* **Invite** a few answers.

Thanks for a great class, everyone!

Ring a bell or chime if you have one.

Flower Breaths

Imagine you have a flower.
Smell the flower for four counts.
Blow the petals for four counts.

Lesson 10
Learn to Say "Fine" in ASL

Slides: 104-115

1. Feelings Check-in and ASL Review

ASL Review
Ask some students to demonstrate how to say happy, sad, excited and hungry in ASL.

ASL
You might say: *T*o*day we are going to learn another way to share a feeling in ASL. We're going to learn how to say "**fine**". Sometimes you don't feel really good or really bad, you just feel fine. What does it feel like in your body when you feel fine? Where do you feel it?*

To show someone that you feel Fine in ASL you can have a pretty happy look on your face - let's practice that. Then you are going to take one hand and spread your fingers out like you are doing Take Five Breathing. Then you'll bring your thumb to touch the middle of your chest so your hand is sticking out from you chest sideways. Let's watch a video of a Peace of Mind student showing how to say "Fine" in ASL. **Fine Video**

Feelings Check-in
You might say: *Now let's do a feelings check in. Take a moment to notice how you are feeling right now. There are lots of ways to feel and you might feel more than one way. Right now I feel happy and excited (or however you feel). Any way that you feel is fine.*

Okay so let's see how you are feeling. You can raise your hand as many times as you want. It's okay to have lots of different feelings.

*Raise your hand or use the sign for "happy" if you are feeling **happy**. Raise your hand or use the sign for "sad" if you are feeling **sad**. Raise your hand or use the sign for "excited" if you are feeling **excited**. Raise your hand or use the sign for "hungry" if you are feeling **hungry**. Raise your hand or use the sign for "fine" if you are feeling **fine**. Raise your hand if you are feeling **angry**. Raise your hand if you are feeling **loved**.*

2. Mindful Moment

You might say: *Who remembers our mindful breathing activity from last time? Yes it was Flower Breathing. Who can show us how to do Flower Breathing?*

You can replay the Marleigh is Mindful video of Flower Breathing, or you can look at it in the book *Marleigh is Mindful.*

Then you can lead the practice: *Let's get into our mindful bodies. Let's close our eyes OR look down. Let's take 3 deep breaths using Flower Breathing.*

Ring the chime when you are finished and say: *Let's listen to the sound of the bell. When you can't hear it anymore you can open your eyes if they are closed or look up.*

Ask: *What did you notice?*

3. Kindness Pals

Assign New Kindness Pals as in Lesson 2

You might say: *Okay it's time to get our new Kindness Pals! There's one important rule of Kindness Pals. Does anybody remember what it is? When I tell you who your Kindness Pal is I want you to say "Okay!" in a nice friendly way and move mindfully to sit with them.*

Kindness Pal Activity: Make the Number

I am going to say a number and you and your Kindness Pal are going to try to show the number on your fingers. So if I say four you could put out two fingers and your Kindness Pal could put out two fingers and that would make four! The one rule is that you can't do the whole number yourself, you have to do it together. Okay? Let's try it!

4. Optional Drawing Activity

Ask students to think about how they feel when they feel fine. Invite them to draw what they look like when they feel fine, prompting them to think about their face, hands, and body movements.

5. Closing

Let's take a moment to think about something kind you could do for your Kindness pal today. You can close your eyes if you want to. **Wait.**

Ask: *Who has an idea of what you might do?* **Invite** a few answers.

Thanks for a great class, everyone!

Ring a bell or chime if you have one.

What do you look like when you feel fine?

Lesson 11
Gratefuls with Peyton

Slides: 116-126

1. Feelings Check-in and ASL Review

ASL Review

Ask if anyone remembers how to say "Fine" in ASL. Ask some students to demonstrate how to say happy, sad, excited, and hungry in ASL.

Feelings Check-in

You might say: *Now let's do a feelings check in. Take a moment to notice how you are feeling right now. There are lots of ways to feel and you might feel more than one way. Right now I feel happy and excited (or however you feel). Any way that you feel is fine.*

Okay so let's see how you are feeling. You can raise your hand as many times as you want. It's okay to have lots of different feelings.

*Raise your hand or use the sign for "happy" if you are feeling **happy**. Raise your hand or use the sign for "sad" if you are feeling **sad**. Raise your hand or use the sign for "excited" if you are feeling **excited**. Raise your hand or use the sign for "hungry" if you are feeling **hungry**. Raise your hand or use the sign for "fine" if you are feeling **fine**. Raise your hand if you are feeling **angry**. Raise your hand if you are feeling **loved**.*

2. Mindful Moment

You might say: *Today we're going to learn more about mindfulness with Marleigh's friend Peyton. Our new practice is called* **_Gratefuls._** *Pause the video when Marleigh says "What would you put in your Gratefuls Box?" and lead the practice.*

Finish the video.

Ask: *What was Peyton grateful for? What did you think of?*

Teaching Tip: *For very young children it can be difficult to come up with an idea during open-ended assignments. Try giving one concrete idea for the whole class, and encourage students to think of something else if they're inclined to do so. That way everyone has an idea and those who are developmentally ready to branch out on their own may do so.*

3. Kindness Pals

Assign New Kindness Pals as in Lesson 2

Okay it's time to get our new Kindness Pals! There's one important rule of Kindness Pals. Does anybody remember what it is? When I tell you who your Kindness Pal is I want you to say "Okay!" in a nice friendly way and move mindfully to sit with them.

Kindness Pal Activity: Gratefuls

Tell your Kindness Pal 3 things you are grateful for. Then you will draw what you are grateful for together. Hand out Coloring Sheet below.

4. Closing

Let's take a moment to think about something kind you could do for your Kindness pal today. You can close your eyes if you want to. **Wait.**

Ask: *Who has an idea of what you might do?* **Invite** a few answers.

Thanks for a great class, everyone!

Ring a bell or chime if you have one.

I am Grateful for

Draw a picture here of something you are grateful for.

My Name: _____

Lesson 12
Learn to Say "Angry" in ASL

Slides: 127-138

1. Feelings Check-in and ASL Review

ASL Review

Ask some students to demonstrate how to say happy, sad, excited, hungry and fine in ASL.

ASL

You might say: *Today we are going to learn another way to share a feeling in ASL. We're going to learn how to say **"angry."** What does it feel like in your body when you are angry? Where do you feel it?*

To show someone that you feel angry in ASL you should have an angry look on your face - let's practice that. Then you are going to take one hand and bend it so it looks kind of like a claw. Or like you are holding an apple in your hand. Then you're going to put that hand in front of your face with your angry expression and move it quickly from left to right. Let's watch a video of a Peace of Mind student showing how to say "angry" in ASL. **Angry Video**

Feelings Check-in

You might say: *Now let's do a feelings check in. Take a moment to notice how you are feeling right now. There are lots of ways to feel and you might feel more than one way. Right now I feel happy and excited (or however you feel). Any way that you feel is fine.*

Okay so let's see how you are feeling. You can raise your hand as many times as you want. It's okay to have lots of different feelings.

*Raise your hand or use the sign for "Happy" if you are feeling **happy**. Raise your hand or use the sign for "sad" if you are feeling **sad**. Raise your hand or use the sign for "excited" if you are feeling **excited**. Raise your hand or use the sign for "hungry" if you are feeling **hungry**. Raise your hand or use the sign for "fine" if you are feeling **fine**. Raise your hand or use the sign for "angry" if you are feeling **angry**. Raise your hand if you are feeling **loved**.*

2. Mindful Moment

You might say: *Who remembers our mindful breathing activity from last time? Yes it was Gratefuls! Can you think of something you are grateful for today?*

You can replay the Marleigh is Mindful video of Gratefuls, or you can look at it in the book *Marleigh is Mindful*.

You can lead the practice: *Let's get into our mindful bodies. Let's close our eyes OR look down. Let's take 3 deep breaths using Flower Breathing and then think of three things that we are grateful for.*

Ring the chime when you are finished and say: *Let's listen to the sound of the bell. When you can't hear it anymore you can open your eyes if they are closed or look up.*

Ask: *What did you notice?*

3. Kindness Pals

Assign New Kindness Pals

You might say: *Okay it's time to get our new Kindness Pals! There's one important rule of Kindness Pals. Does anybody remember what it is? When I tell you who your Kindness Pal is I want you to say "Okay!" in a nice friendly way and move mindfully to sit with them.*

Kindness Pal Activity: Kindness Pal Challenge
I am going to set a timer for 30 seconds and in that time you and your Kindness pal are going to find out how many things you have in common (how many things are the same about you). Try to count them. Okay? Let's try it!

Share out if there is time.

4. Optional Drawing Activity

Ask students to think about how they feel when they feel angry. Invite them to draw what they look like when they feel angry, prompting them to think about their face, hands, and body movements.

5. Closing

Let's take a moment to think about something kind you could do for your Kindness pal today. You can close your eyes if you want to. **Wait.**

Ask*: Who has an idea of what you might do?* **Invite** a few answers.

Thanks for a great class, everyone!

Ring a bell or chime if you have one.

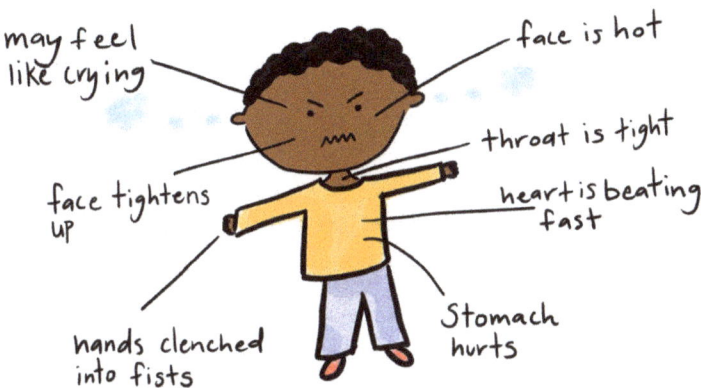

may feel like crying

face is hot

throat is tight

face tightens up

heart is beating fast

hands clenched into fists

Stomach hurts

What do you look like when you feel angry?

|

Lesson 13
Make Up Your Own Breaths

Slides: 139-150

1. Feelings Check-in and ASL Review

ASL Review

Ask some students to demonstrate how to say happy, sad, excited, hungry, fine and angry in ASL.

Feelings Check-in

You might say: *Now let's do a feelings check in. Take a moment to notice how you are feeling right now. There are lots of ways to feel and you might feel more than one way. Right now I feel happy and excited* (or however you feel). *Any way that you feel is fine.*

Okay so let's see how you are feeling. You can raise your hand as many times as you want. It's okay to have lots of different feelings.

*Raise your hand or use the sign for "happy" if you are feeling **happy**. Raise your hand or use the sign for "sad" if you are feeling **sad**. Raise your hand or use the sign for "excited" if you are feeling **excited**. Raise your hand or use the sign for "hungry" if you are feeling **hungry**. Raise your hand or use the sign for "fine" if you are feeling **fine**. Raise your hand or use the sign for "angry" if you are feeling **angry**. Raise your hand if you are feeling **loved**.*

2. Mindful Moment

You might say: *Today we're going to be making up our own ways of doing mindful breathing. First, let's watch a video featuring a girl named Silvia who made up her own way of doing mindful breathing called* Wave Breathing.

Let's get into our mindful bodies. Let's close our eyes OR look down. Let's take 3 deep breaths using Wave Breaths.

Ring the chime when you are finished and say: *Let's listen to the sound of the bell. When you can't hear it anymore you can open your eyes if they are closed or look up.*

Ask: *What did you notice?*

3. Kindness Pals

Assign New Kindness Pals

You might say: *Okay it's time to get our new Kindness Pals! There's one important rule of Kindness Pals. Does anybody remember what it is? When I tell you who your Kindness Pal is, I want you to say "Okay!" in a nice friendly way.*

Kindness Pal Activity: Teach Your Kindness Pal Your Way of Breathing
Take a moment to create your own way of doing mindful breathing and then teach it to your Kindness Pal. Share a few with the class if there is time.

4. Optional Coloring / Drawing Activity

Ask students to think about times when they could use Wave Breathing. Have them color in the Coloring Sheet below. They may also draw their own way of breathing on the second Coloring Sheet.

5. Closing

Let's take a moment to think about something kind you could do for your Kindness pal today. You can close your eyes if you want to. **Wait.**
Ask*: Who has an idea of what you might do?* **Invite** a few answers.
Thanks for a great class, everyone!
Ring a bell or chime if you have one.

Wave Breaths

Breathe in and out moving
your arms like a wave.

TeachPeaceofMind.org

Create Your Own Breath

Lesson 14
Learn to Say "Loved" in ASL

Slides: 151-162

1. Feelings Check-in and ASL Review

ASL Review
Ask some students to demonstrate how to say happy, sad, excited, hungry, fine and angry in ASL.

ASL
You might say: *Today we are going to learn another way to share a feeling in ASL. We're going to learn how to say "**loved."** What does it feel like in your body when you feel loved? Where do you feel it?*

To show someone that you feel loved in ASL you should have a happy look on your face - let's practice that. Then you are going to take your hands and cross them across your chest. Let's watch a video of a Peace of Mind student showing how to say "Loved" in ASL. **Loved Video**

Feelings Check-in
You might say: *Now let's do a feelings check in. Take a moment to notice how you are feeling right now. There are lots of ways to feel and you might feel more than one way. Right now I feel happy and excited (or however you feel). Any way that you feel is fine.*

Okay so let's see how you are feeling. You can raise your hand as many times as you want. It's okay to have lots of different feelings.

*Raise your hand or use the sign for "happy" if you are feeling **happy**. Raise your hand or use the sign for "sad" if you are feeling **sad**. Raise your hand or use the sign for "excited" if you are feeling **excited**. Raise your hand or use the sign for "hungry" if you are feeling **hungry**. Raise your hand or use the sign for "fine" if you are feeling **fine**. Raise your hand or use the sign for "angry" if you are feeling **angry**. Raise your hand or use the sign for "loved" if you are feeling **loved**.*

2. Mindful Moment

You might say: *Who remembers our mindful breathing activity from last time? Yes it was Wave Breathing! Can anybody show us how to do Wave Breathing?*

You can replay the Wave Breathing video and then lead the practice: *Let's get into our mindful bodies. Let's close our eyes OR look down. Let's take 3 deep breaths using Wave Breathing.*

Ring the chime when you are finished and say: *Let's listen to the sound of the bell. When you can't hear it anymore you can open your eyes if they are closed or look up.*

Ask: *What did you notice?*

3. Kindness Pals

Assign New Kindness Pals

You might say: *Okay it's time to get our new Kindness Pals! There's one important rule of Kindness Pals. Does anybody remember what it is? When I tell you who your Kindness Pal is I want you to say "Okay!" in a nice friendly way.*

Kindness Pal Activity: Kindness Pal Challenge

I am going to set a timer for 30 seconds and in that time you and your Kindness pal are going to find out how many things you have in common - or how many things are the same about you. Try to count them. Okay? Let's try it!

4. Optional Drawing Activity

Ask students to think about how they feel when they feel loved. Invite them to draw what they look like when they feel loved, prompting them to think about their face, hands, and body movements.

5. Closing

Let's take a moment to think about something kind you could do for your Kindness pal today. You can close your eyes if you want to. **Wait.**
Ask: *Who has an idea of what you might do?* **Invite** a few answers.
Thanks for a great class, everyone!
Ring a bell or chime if you have one.

What do you look like when you feel loved?

Peace of Mind®

Lesson 15
Heartfulness

Slides: 163-174

Note: watch this video if you want to see an example of this activity.

1. Feelings Check-in and ASL Review

ASL Review

Ask some students to demonstrate how to say happy, sad, excited, hungry, fine, angry and loved in ASL.

Feelings Check-in

You might say: *Now let's do a feelings check in. Take a moment to notice how you are feeling right now. There are lots of ways to feel and you might feel more than one way. Right now I feel happy and excited (or however you feel). Any way that you feel is fine.*

Okay so let's see how you are feeling. You can raise your hand as many times as you want. It's okay to have lots of different feelings.

Raise your hand or use the sign for "happy" if you are feeling **happy**. *Raise your hand or use the sign for "sad" if you are feeling* **sad**. *Raise your hand or use the sign for "excited" if you are feeling* **excited**. *Raise your hand or use the sign for "hungry" if you are feeling* **hungry**. *Raise your hand or use the sign for "fine" if you are feeling* **fine**. *Raise your hand or use the sign for "angry" if you are feeling* **angry**. *Raise your hand or use the sign for "loved" if you are feeling* **loved**.

2. Mindful Moment

You might say: *Today we're going to be learning one more way of doing mindfulness called Heartfulness. First let's watch a video with the voice of Marleigh's cousin Stella doing Heartfulness.*

Let's try Heartfulness together.
Let's get into our mindful bodies. Let's close our eyes OR look down.
Let's take 3 deep breaths using Wave Breaths.

Let's think of somebody that we love and see every day and think "May you be Happy. May you be Healthy. May you be Peaceful."
Next let's think about ourselves and think "May I be Happy. May I be Healthy. May I be Peaceful."
Now let's think of everyone in this class and think "May we be Happy. May we be healthy. May we be Peaceful."

Ring the chime when you are finished. *Let's listen to the sound of the bell. When you can't hear it anymore, open your eyes if they are closed or look up.*

Ask: *What did you notice?*

3. Kindness Pals

Assign New Kindness Pals

You might say: *Okay it's time to get our new Kindness Pals! There's one important rule of Kindness Pals. Does anybody remember what it is? When I tell you who your Kindness Pal is I want you to say "Okay!" in a nice friendly way.*

Kindness Pal Activity: Kindness Chain

You might say: *This is our last Peace of Mind class and so it's a great time to show some kindness to each other. Today we are going to make a Kindness Chain. The first step is to gather into a circle.*

We are going to go around the circle and I'd like you to say something kind about the person sitting to your right. For example, I might say, "Cheryl, you are an awesome friend."

Cheryl might say "Thanks!" and then turn to the person on her right and say, "Harry, you are really good at building things."

And we'll go around the circle like that. Every once in a while when we play this game somebody can't think of anything to say—even if they are sitting next to their best friend! If that happens to you, don't worry. Just say, "I need some help," and I will choose a volunteer to say something kind about that person. Then we'll continue going around the circle.

When we're done, we'll go around the circle in the other direction.

This is a chance to use the power of our words to make people feel really good so let's try hard to take it seriously and make sure that everybody feels good. Ready to start?

4. Optional Coloring Activity

Ask students to think about times when they could use Heartfulness. Have them color in the Coloring Sheet below.

5. Closing

This is our last class together. I hope that you enjoyed learning more about mindfulness, kindness, and how to work out our conflicts peacefully. The world needs lots of kind, mindful people. Now you have some tools to help you go out into the world and make it a more peaceful place. I hope you will!

Thank you so much!

Heartfulness

Think kind thoughts for yourself, somebody else, or the whole world.

TeachPeaceofMind.org

Peace of Mind®

About Linda Ryden, Author

Linda Ryden is the author of seven mindfulness-based children's books published by Cherry Lake Publishing and Peace of Mind Inc. Linda is the founder and Creative Director of Peace of Mind Inc. and creator of the Peace of Mind Program and author of the Peace of Mind Curriculum Series, a cutting-edge combination of mindfulness-based social-emotional learning, conflict resolution and social justice for Early Childhood through Middle School. Linda served as the full-time Peace Teacher at Lafayette Elementary School, Washington DC's largest public elementary school from 2003 to 2023, teaching Peace of Mind classes to more than 700 students every week.

Linda's work has been featured in *The Washington Post*, *Washingtonian Magazine*, *Washington Parent*, *Washington Family*, *Teaching Tolerance*, and *Edutopia*, among others. Linda was a keynote speaker at the National Network of State Teachers of the Year conference and a featured speaker at the National Education Association Foundation Symposium, and has received a Commendation for Educational Innovation from the DC Board of Education.

Linda lives in Washington D.C. with her husband Jeremiah Cohen, owner of Bullfrog Bagels, and their dog Phoebe.

In that small but growing band of peace educators, Linda Ryden stands out. The glistening ideas and stories in these pages are sure to open minds and stir hearts, in much the way that has been happening all these years with the children in her classrooms.

— Colman McCarthy, Founder of The Center for Teaching Peace

Bibliography

Bradshaw, C. P. (2015). Translating research to practice in bullying prevention. American Psychologist, 70 (4), 322-332.

Breeding, K., & Harrison, J. (2007). Connected and Respected: Lessons from the Resolving Conflict Creatively Program. Cambridge, Mass.: Educators for Social Responsibility.

Durlak, J. A., Weissberg, R. P., Dymnicki, A. B., Taylor, R. D. & Schellinger, K. B. (2011). The impact of enhancing students' social and emotional learning: A meta-analysis of school-based universal interventions. Child Development, 82(1): 405–432.

Hanson, R. (2015). Hardwiring Happiness. Random House USA.

Jennings, P. (2015). Mindfulness for teachers: Simple skills for peace and productivity in the classroom. The Norton Series on the Social Neuroscience of Education.

Jennings, P. A. (2019). The Trauma-Sensitive Classroom: Building Resilience with Compassionate Teaching. New York: W.W. Norton & Company.

Lantieri, Linda. "How SEL and Mindfulness Can Work Together." Greater Good. April 7, 2015. Accessed September 28, 2015. http://greatergood.berkeley.edu/article/item/how_social_emotional_learning_and_mindfulness_can_work_together.

Learning Heroes, Developing Life Skills in Children: A Road Map for Communicating with Parents, https://bealearninghero.org/parent-mindsets/ September 2018

O'Brennan, L., & Bradshaw, C. (2013). School Climate: A Research Brief. A report prepared for the National Education Association, Washington, DC.

Rechtschaffen, D., & Kabat-Zinn PhD, J. (2014). The Way of Mindful Education: Cultivating Well-being in Teachers and Students. Norton Books in Education. Schonert-Reichl, K. A., & Lawlor, M. S. (2010). The effects of a mindfulness-based education program on pre-and early adolescents' well-being and social and emotional competence. Mindfulness, 1(3), 137-151.

Schonert-Reichl, K. A., Oberle, E., Lawlor, M. S., Abbott, D., Thomson, K., Oberlander, T. F., & Diamond, A. (2015). Enhancing cognitive and social–emotional development through a simple-to-administer mindfulness-based school program for elementary school children: A randomized controlled trial. Developmental Psychology, 51(1), 52-66.

Seppala, E., Simon-Thomas, E., Brown, S. L., Worline, M. C., Cameron, C. D., & Doty, J. R. (2017). The Oxford Handbook of Compassion Science. New York, NY: Oxford University Press.

Siegel, D. J., & Bryson, T. P. (2012). The Whole-Brain Child. London: Constable & Robinson.

Simmons, Dena (2019), Why We Can't Afford Whitewashed Social-Emotional Learning Retrieved from http://www.ascd.org/publications/newsletters/education_update/apr19/vol61/num04

Srinivasan, M. (2014). Teach, Breathe, Learn: Mindfulness in and out of the Classroom. Berkeley, CA: Parallax Press.

Treleaven, David (2018). Trauma-Sensitive Mindfulness: Practices for Safe and Transformative Healing. New York: W. W. Norton & Company.

Weare, K. (2013). Developing mindfulness with children and young people: A review of the evidence and policy context. Journal of Children's Services, 8(2), 141-153.

Zoogman, S., Goldberg, S.B., Hoyt, W.T., & Miller, L. (2015). Mindfulness interventions with youth: A meta-analysis. Mindfulness, 6, 290 - 302.

Zenner, C., Hermleben-Kurz, S., & Walach, H. (2014). Mindfulness-based interventions in schools: A systematic review and meta-analysis. Frontiers in Psychology, 5, article 603.

Appreciation

Peace of Mind is based in our community, and we are so lucky to have the support and guidance and help of so many wonderful people. We are grateful to Mike Di Marco, Valentina Gabrielli and the teachers and staff of Horizons Greater Washington for inspiring us to create this curriculum and being our first pilot program in summer 2024. A fantastic group of educators in the DC area and beyond piloted the Flex Curriculum during the 24-25 school year and provided helpful feedback. This curriculum wouldn't exist without many wonderful friends of Peace of Mind including Kelly Gilstrap, Jillian Diesner, Jodi Ferrier, Elie Goldman, Jennifer Greene, our friends at Metamer Studios, and the students who helped to create the amazing ASL and mindfulness videos. As always, we are able to do what we do at Peace of Mind thanks to the support of very generous foundations and kind individual donors! Thank you!!

Notes